KEEP OUT OF THE KITCHEN, MUM

KEEP OUT OF THE KITCHEN, MUM

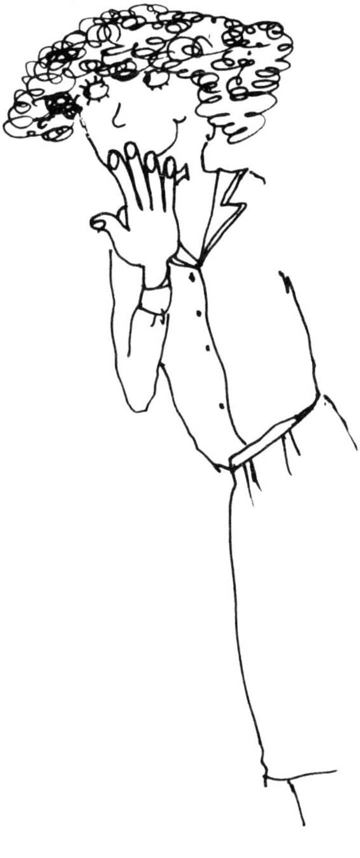

JILL COX

ANDRE DEUTSCH

For Hannah and Tom
who keep in the kitchen
and David who kept cool

First published 1984 by
André Deutsch Limited
105–106 Great Russell Street London WC1B 3LJ
This edition published in 1991 by
André Deutsch Limited

ISBN 0-233-98632 4

Printed in Great Britain by
the Hollen Street Press, Slough, Bucks

CONTENTS

Author's note:

There is a possibility that raw eggs may contain salmonella, which can make people ill and vulnerable groups such as the sick, very young, very old, pregnant mothers and those with immune deficiencies should avoid those recipes containing raw eggs.

HOW TO USE THIS BOOK

If you've never cooked before, choose a simple recipe. These are all marked  at the top of the page and are guaranteed easy. Read the recipe through from beginning to end. Any cookery words you don't understand, look up on pages 8 to 11.

Before you start, make sure you have all the ingredients and equipment listed. The measurements are given in metric and imperial; make sure you *always* stick to one or the other. Check on pages 12 to 17 for descriptions and pictures of all the kitchen utensils.

Next, put on an apron, roll your sleeves up and give your hands a good scrub. Now you can start assembling all the equipment and measuring out the ingredients.

After this, follow each instruction carefully. Each new step is on a new line, but ask an adult if you are not quite sure what to do.

Don't forget to wash everything up when you've finished and clear up anything you might have spilt. This way, everyone will be pleased. You can do your cooking on your own and Mum and Dad won't interfere or complain afterwards.

COOKERY WORDS

BAKE: Cook inside the oven.
BASTE: Brush or spoon liquid from the roasting pan over food as it cooks.

BEAT: Make a mixture smooth by beating with a wooden spoon or hand whisk, with a circular movement. You can also beat with an electric whisk. This is much faster, but don't use electrical gadgets without asking permission.

BIND: Gather moistened ingredients together in a ball by using your fingers or a wooden spoon.
BLEND: Mix two or more ingredients together till smooth.
BOIL: Heat liquid in a saucepan till it's bubbling and steaming.

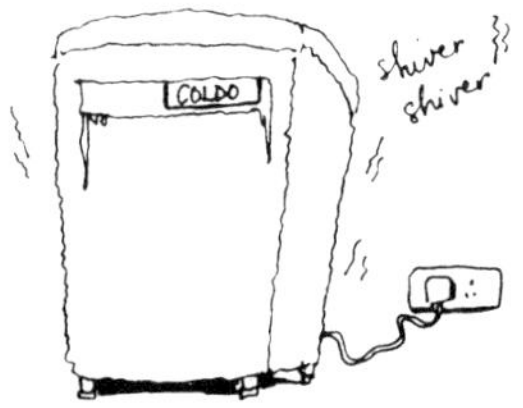

CHILL: Cool something down thoroughly in the fridge.

CHOP: Cut into small pieces (the recipes say what size).

COMBINE: Stir ingredients together.

CREAM: Beat butter or margarine with sugar till the grittiness of the sugar disappears and the mixture is soft, light and creamy.

DICE: Cut food into small even cubes (the recipes say what size).

FOLD: Mix one mixture into another by carefully turning them over together with a metal spoon rather than stirring.

FRY: Cook in hot fat or oil in a pan on top of the cooker.

GARNISH: Decorate food with thin lemon slices, chopped herbs, nuts, etc. to make it look specially appetising.

GLAZE: Brush with beaten egg or milk before cooking to give a golden shine after cooking.

GRATE: Shred foods like cheese, chocolate, vegetables etc. by rubbing them on the sides of a grater.

GREASE: Wipe the base and sides of a baking tin or mould with oil or fat to stop what you're cooking sticking to the tin.

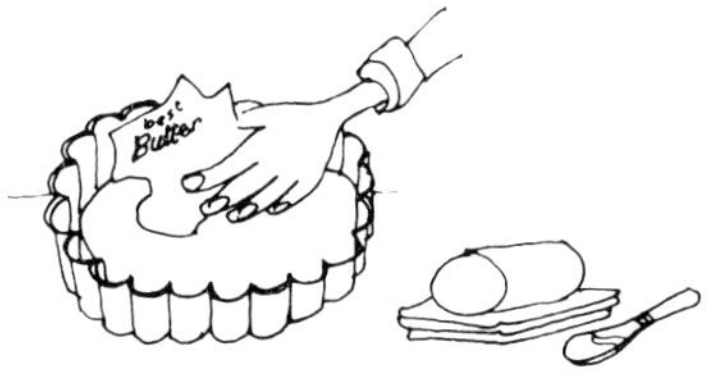

INGREDIENTS: All the food items listed in a recipe.

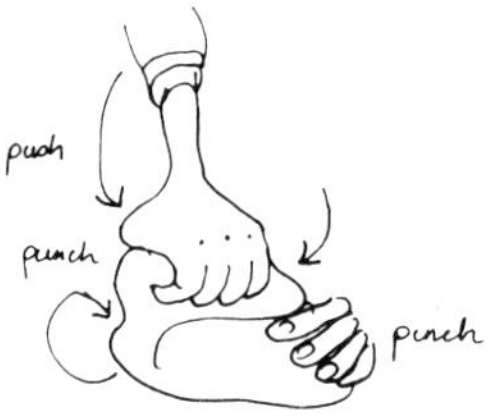

KNEAD: Fold, turn over and push down dough during breadmaking to make it smooth and elastic.

MELT: Make something solid like butter, margarine or chocolate into a liquid, usually by heating it.

PEEL: Remove the skin of fruit or vegetables with a sharp knife or potato peeler.

PIPE: Make pretty swirls and shapes out of icing or whipped cream by squeezing it out of a piping bag with a fluted nozzle. A plain nozzle is used for straight lines, writing people's names or messages.

PRE-HEAT: Switch on the oven at the temperature you need before you start your preparations. This makes sure the oven will be at the right temperature when you are ready.

ROLL OUT: Use a rolling pin dusted with flour to flatten a piece of pastry to the thickness you need.

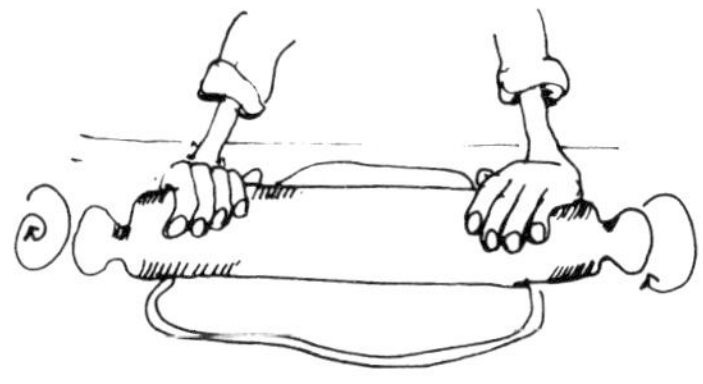

RUB IN: Start off with a bowl of flour with cubes of fat in it, and end up with it looking like breadcrumbs. Use your fingertips to rub little pieces of fat through the flour until they get smaller and smaller. You should lift your hands out of the bowl while you do this to keep the mixture cool and let as much air in as possible.

SIEVE: Push powdery food like flour or icing sugar through a sieve, using a spoon, to get rid of all the lumps.

SIMMER: Cook something in liquid with the heat turned down very low so you can only see the odd bubble breaking on the surface.

WHIP: Use a hand or electric whisk to make egg whites or cream stiff, and full of air.

WHISK: The same as above but beat until the mixture is just frothing and not stiff. You can do this with a fork too.

EQUIPMENT

BAKING SHEET: a big flat metal sheet for cooking biscuits and pastry.

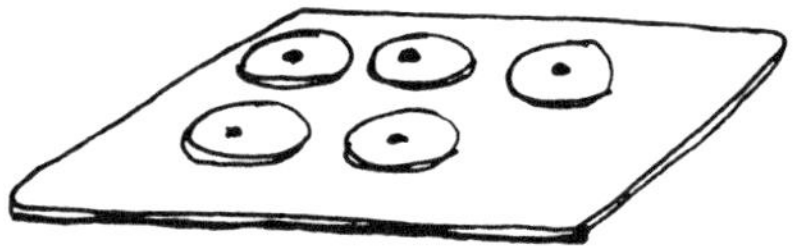

BAKING TIN: for roasting.

CASSEROLE: a large ovenproof pot with a properly fitting lid for cooking stews in the oven. Some are flameproof which means you can use them on a gas or electric hob too, but make absolutely certain the one you are using *is* flameproof before putting it on the hob.

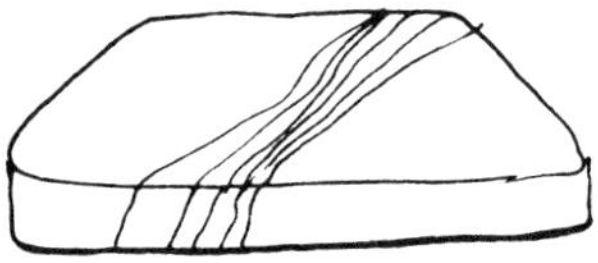

CHOPPING BOARD: a thick wooden or plastic board which protects tables and worktops when you're cutting or chopping. Use the back of the bread board if you haven't got a special board for chopping.

COLANDER: looks like a tin helmet with holes in — used for straining things.

CUTTERS: for cutting shapes from rolled out pastry or biscuit dough.

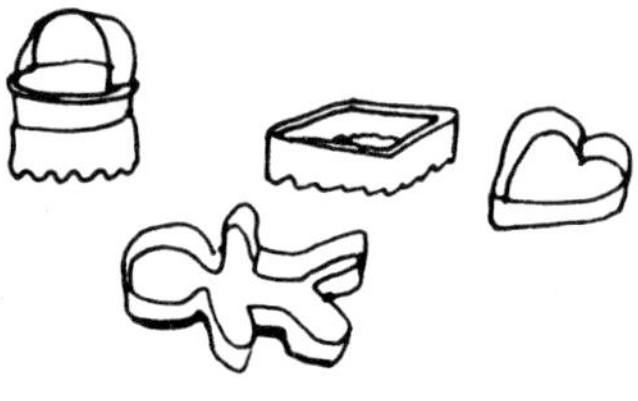

DRAINING SPOON: a large spoon with holes in. Used for lifting and draining things which have cooked in liquid.

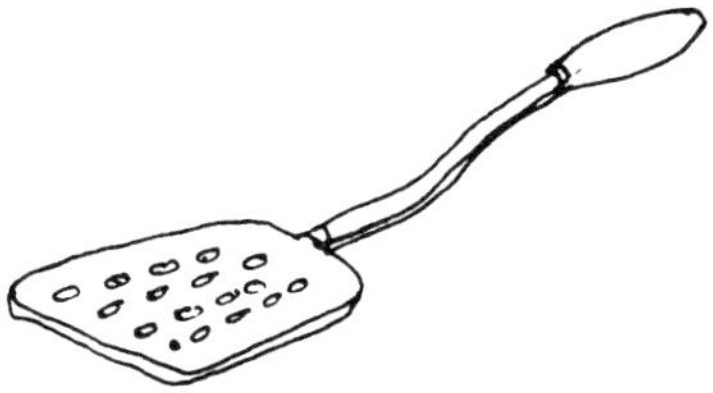

FISH SLICE: used for lifting fragile items from baking sheets or out of frying pans. The holes allow for draining.

FRYING PANS: a small one and a large one — non-stick are easiest to clean.

GARLIC SQUEEZER: special gadget for pressing fat cloves of garlic through small holes to give you tiny pieces of garlic.

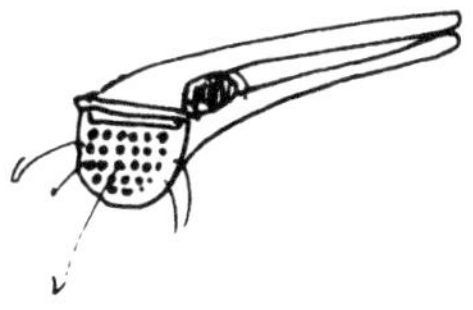

GRATER: usually has different sized holes on three sides for grating things like cheese or chocolate into small, smaller or smallest curls. The fourth side may have a slicer useful for cutting thin slices of cucumber or potato for crisps.

LOOSE BOTTOMED CAKE TIN: a round cake tin with a loose base. This makes getting the cake out a lot easier.

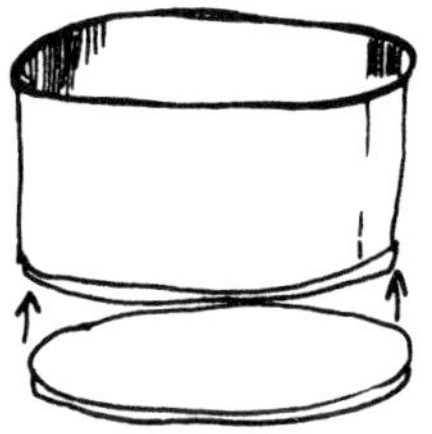

MEASURING JUG: for measuring liquid ingredients.

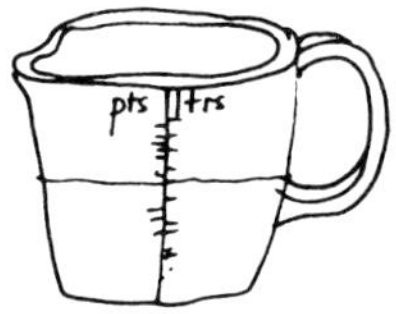

MIXING BOWL: a bowl large enough to turn everything over in without spilling the ingredients over the sides.

MOULDS: for making jellies and other cold puddings in pretty shapes. Also used for savoury moulds like fish mousse.

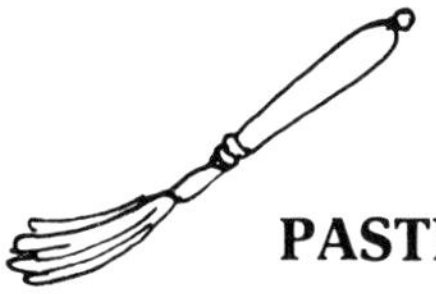

PASTRY BRUSH: for painting glaze on pastry before cooking.

PALETTE KNIFE: long, narrow, flat, bendy blade with both sides blunt and the end rounded. Used for lifting or mixing.

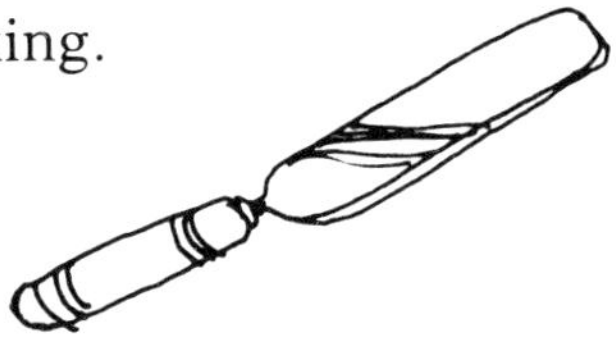

PATTY TIN: a tin which usually has 9 or 12 round dents in to make tarts, cakes or Yorkshire puddings.

POACHING PAN: a special shallow pan containing saucer shaped hollows to give you perfect poached eggs with neat whites.

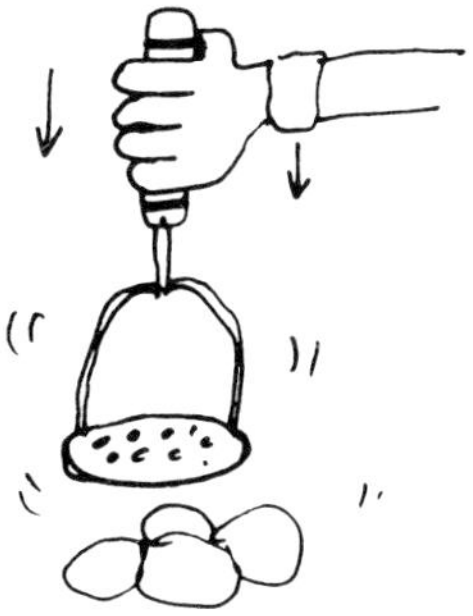

POTATO MASHER: makes fast work of mashing cooked potatoes or raw bananas.

ROLLING PIN: for rolling pastry flat. Always flour the rolling pin and the work surface first to stop pastry sticking. Also useful for crushing nuts, crisps and crumbs. Put them in a paper bag, then roll firmly.

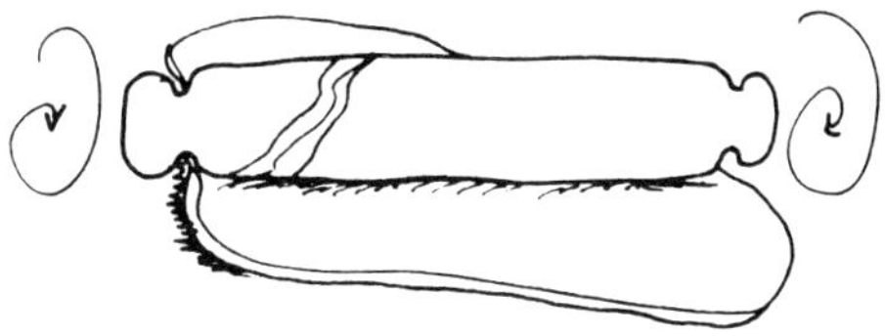

SAUCEPANS: several different sizes are useful. Non-stick are best.

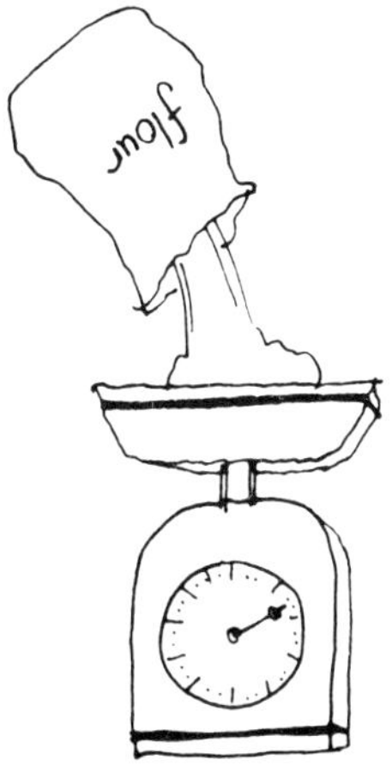

SCALES: for measuring dry ingredients by weight. Some old scales have imperial measurements only — in ounces and pounds. All the recipes in this book have both metric and imperial amounts.
When making any dish, stick to one or the other.

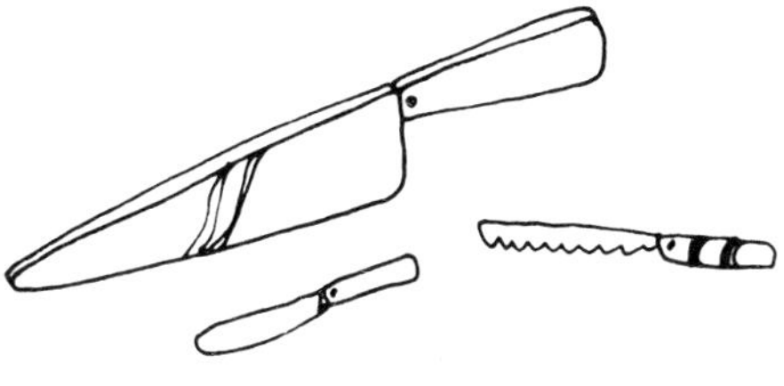

SHARP KNIVES: it is essential to have sharp knives and to be very careful how you use them. Always cut away from, *never* towards, yourself. Always hold the knife point and blade downwards. Always use a proper chopping board.

SIEVE: made of metal or nylon. Used for sifting powdery ingredients to make sure there are no lumps, or for straining liquids with very fine lumps which would fall through the holes of a colander.

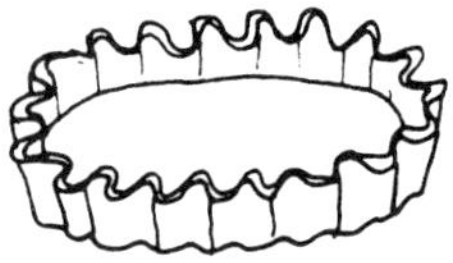

TART TIN: a frilly edged shallow tin for making tarts or quiches.

TIN OPENER: the sort you clip on to the rim of a tin and turn a key is the easiest to use.

WHISKS: there are three sorts. Rotary ones which you work by turning the handle, balloon ones made of wire which you use by beating with a circular movement, or electric ones which you only use with permission.

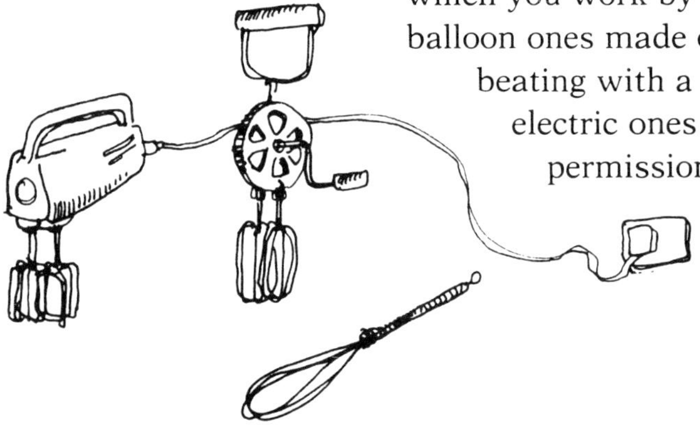

WIRE RACK: a metal grid for putting cakes, pastries or biscuits on when you take them out of the oven; so they can cool down all over and the bottom won't go soggy.

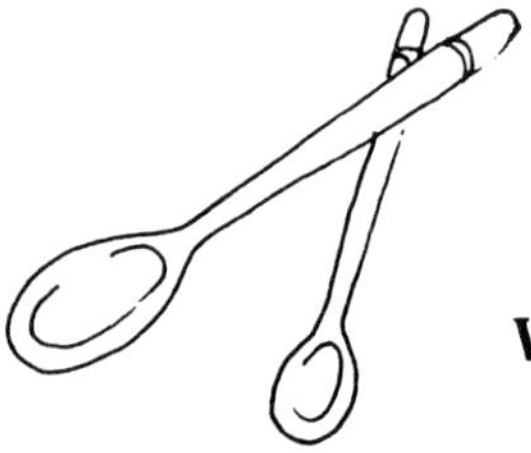

WOODEN SPOONS: for mixing, beating and stirring.

MEASUREMENTS

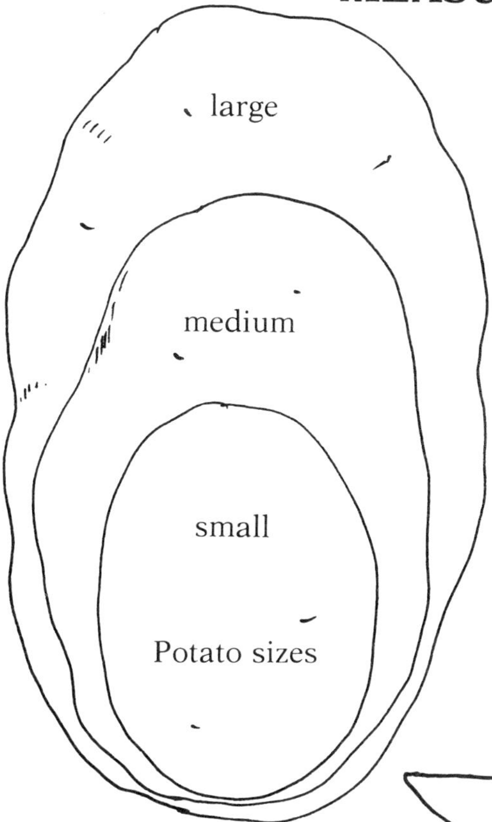

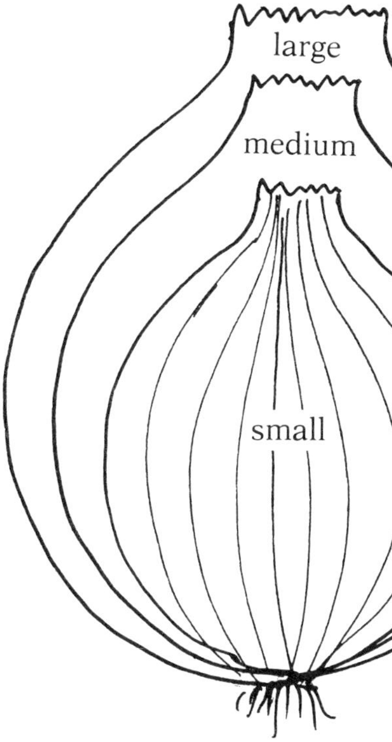

Onion sizes

bite-sized chunk

shake of pepper

pinch of salt

OVEN HEAT

GAS	F	C	
¼	225	110	
½	250	120	
1	275	140	Cool
2	300	150	
3	325	160	Moderate
4	350	180	
5	375	190	Hottish
6	400	200	
7	425	220	Hot
8	450	230	
9	475	240	Very hot

HELPFUL ADVICE

KITCHEN LORE

1. ALWAYS ask adults if you can use the food you need for your own cooking, in case they bought it for something special.
2. ALWAYS make sure your ingredients are clean and fresh.
3. ALWAYS ask adults if you can use a piece of equipment, especially electrical equipment, in case you need supervision; some things are quite tricky to use.
4. If you use electrical equipment, make sure you switch it off at the plug the minute you finish using it, not just at the machine. Also remember that it is dangerous to touch electric switches with wet hands.
5. Do your own washing up and PUT THINGS AWAY.
6. Wipe the cooker clean.
7. Clear up spills on the kitchen floor, in case you slip over or cause anyone else in the family to have an accident.
8. Use knives with great care. Always cut away from you on the chopping board. This way you won't slice up your hands and won't ruin the kitchen worktops.
9. Always use oven mitts to lift hot things out of a hot oven.
10. Keep saucepan handles turned away from the front of the oven to avoid accidentally knocking them.

COOKING LORE

1. You don't always need to weigh things. Often they come in packs with the weight printed on.

2. Don't peel vegetables unless you really have to because they're damaged or bruised. A lot of the goodness is in, or just under, the skin. Just scrub them well.

3. Wash lettuces in cold water, then blot them dry with kitchen paper. If you leave them wet you will dilute any salad dressing.

4. Never peel mushrooms. Cut a thin slice off the bottom of the stalk, then wash and dry them before use.

5. Pastry is easier to roll out if you wrap it in clingfilm and chill it for half an hour before use.

6. Freeze fruit juice in the ice tray to cool down summer drinks without diluting them.

7. Sprinkle cut fruit with lemon juice to stop it going brown.

8. Be extra careful when separating egg whites from yolks. If you get a speck of yolk in the whites they won't whip stiff.

9. *How food looks* is very important. Always arrange things so they look appetising on the serving plate. Slices of cucumber or tomato, or sprigs of parsley, mustard & cress or lemon slices or nuts are called garnishes when you use them to decorate food. Cakes and biscuits look attractive on a doily.

10. Make chicken or beef stock from a cube, following the instructions on the packet.

USEFUL RECIPES

Hot Hands Pastry

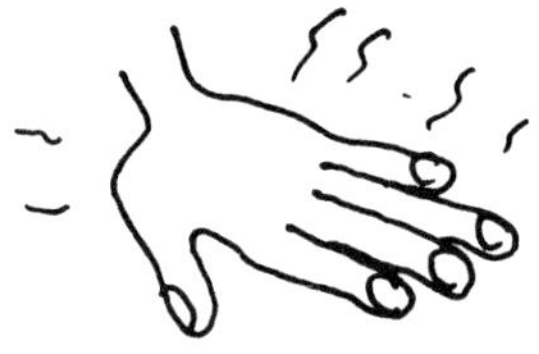

One of the reasons it's hard to make light and crisp pastry is because it gets too warm while it's being made, usually from too much contact with hot hands. This recipe is practically fool proof. Even adults who think they can't make pastry will find it amazingly good.

EQUIPMENT

small bowl, knives, tablespoon, sieve, clingfilm

INGREDIENTS

8 level tablespoons sifted plain flour

4 level tablespoons butter or hard margarine

2 tablespoons water

pinch of salt

more flour for sprinkling on the work top

METHOD

1. Put the flour and salt into a bowl
2. Add the butter or margarine cut into small pieces.
3. Using two knives cut the butter or margarine into smaller and smaller pieces in the flour till the mix looks roughly like crumbs.
4. Pour in the water, then gather the dough together with your hands.
5. Liberally sprinkle the work surface with flour (if you used plain white flour to make the pastry you could try using wholewheat to sprinkle on the top, this gives it an interesting texture).
6. Heap the dough out on to the flour, then work it quickly into a ball. Wrap in clingfilm, then chill in the fridge for 15 minutes. Easy isn't it? Rolling out won't be difficult either.

Mayonnaise

A dreamy savoury sauce which adults, for some reason, are nervous of trying. It's used for chunky salads like potato or pasta, salads with meat or fish or mixed chopped fruit, celery and nuts. Some people like it on just about anything, including beefburgers. Mayonnaise is made from raw eggs (see Author's Note on page 6.) so store it in a cool place. Do not keep it too long – this should be no problem at all.

EQUIPMENT

teaspoon(teasp), measuring jug, bowl, hand whisk or electric beater

INGREDIENTS

1	egg yolk	1
1 heaped teasp	mild French mustard	1 heaped teasp
150ml	salad oil	¼ pint
1 teasp	red or white wine vinegar *or* lemon juice	1 teasp
	salt and pepper	

METHOD

1. Put the egg yolk in a bowl with the mustard, a pinch of salt and 3 good shakes of pepper.
2. Measure the oil into a small jug.
3. Using a wire whisk or an electric beater, quickly mix the yolk and mustard together, then add a drip of oil. Beat this well in. Then add another drip. This is the secret of making mayonnaise — you must add the oil drip by drip and beat each drip in well. If you pour in too much at a time the sauce won't go thick.
4. As soon as the mayonnaise is obviously thicker, you can add the oil a little more than a drip at a time, but only add more when you're sure the last amount you mixed has been properly absorbed.
5. Continue beating till all the oil is used up.
6. Stir in the vinegar.

You can add extra flavour if you fancy it with a pinch of curry powder, a teaspoon of finely chopped herbs or finely grated lemon or orange rind.

Vinaigrette or French Dressing

This is a thin salad dressing used with salad vegetables such as lettuce, cucumber, tomatoes, peppers, spring onions and other roots or leaves shredded finely, or sometimes with salads made from rice or beans.

EQUIPMENT

Teaspoon, tablespoon, screwtop jar

INGREDIENTS

1 teaspoon mild French mustard
1 tablespoon red or white wine vinegar
4 tablespoons salad oil
pinch of salt
3 good shakes of black pepper
or 4 grinds of fresh black pepper

METHOD

Put all the ingredients into a screw top jar and give it a good shake. You can vary the flavour by adding a teaspoon of lemon juice for a sharper dressing, some very finely chopped herbs or a crushed clove of garlic.

FOOD FOR MONDAY — FRIDAY

Breakfast

Muesli

You've heard dentists nagging about how bad sugar is for your teeth, and they mean the sugar you put on cornflakes as well as the sugar you eat in sweets and cakes. Make up your own muesli combination and you'll find you use far less sugar. Choose a big jar with a screw top and mix up enough for a week at a time.

EQUIPMENT

mug, tablespoon, bowl, large screw top jar

INGREDIENTS

4 mugfuls porridge oats
2 mugfuls wheatflakes
1 mugful raisins
2 tablespoons brown sugar
2 tablespoons chopped hazelnuts
pinch of salt

METHOD

Mix together in a bowl, transfer to a jar and screw the lid on tight. Serve with sliced bananas or sliced apples, cored but not peeled. Eat with milk or orange juice. For a change try it mixed with creamy yoghurt.

THE EGG

Eggs are one of nature's wonder foods. They're good for protein filled traditional English breakfasts — but only eat them 2 or 3 times a week, and always make sure they are fresh.

BOILED EGGS

SOFT BOILED (set whites and runny yolks)

You probably have a special saucepan for boiled eggs. If not, don't use an aluminium pan as it will go black on the inside.

EQUIPMENT

small saucepan, draining spoon, knife, teaspoon, egg cups

INGREDIENTS

1 egg per person

buttered toast

METHOD

1. Using a draining spoon, lower the eggs carefully, one at a time into a saucepan of boiling water. Bring the water back to the boil.
2. Turn the heat down a little to avoid fast boiling and too much splashing and cook for 4 minutes. Turn off the heat.
3. Remove the eggs from the water with the draining spoon and crack the tops with a teaspoon to stop them cooking any more.
4. Serve with buttered toast fingers.

HARD BOILED (hard whites and yolks)

EQUIPMENT

small saucepan, draining spoon, teaspoon, knife, small bowl or egg cup

INGREDIENTS

1 egg per person

buttered toast (if you're eating the eggs hot)

METHOD

1. and 2. as for soft boiled, but cook for ten minutes.
3. Remove the eggs from the pan with a draining spoon and put immediately into a bowl of cold water if you are going to eat them cold. This stops a black line forming between the yolk and the white. If you're having them hot, eat straightaway, with buttered toast fingers.

POACHED (1)

EQUIPMENT

poaching pan, knife, cup, plate

INGREDIENTS

1 egg per person

butter

buttered toast

METHOD

1. Fill the bottom of a poaching pan with water and bring to the boil.
2. Put a small knob of butter to melt in a poaching hollow.
3. Break an egg into a cup, then carefully pour it into a poaching hollow. Repeat to make as many poached eggs as you need.
4. Put the lid on the pan and simmer for 3 minutes.
5. Remove from the pan and serve on buttered toast.

Poached (2)

If you don't have a poaching pan, there is another way to make poached eggs, but you must use very new eggs for this method so the whites of the eggs don't spread all over the pan.

EQUIPMENT

frying pan, teaspoon, knife, cup, draining spoon, plate

INGREDIENTS

1 egg per person

2 teaspoons vinegar

buttered toast

METHOD

1. Half fill a frying pan with water, add the vinegar then bring to the boil. Turn down to simmering.
2. Break the eggs one at a time into a cup, then gently slip them into the water. Only cook two eggs at a time.
3. Cook for 2 — 3 minutes basting with water till the whites are set and the yolks are sealed and cloudy.
5. Lift out one by one carefully with a draining spoon.
6. Serve on buttered toast.

Scrambled Eggs

EQUIPMENT

Small bowl, teaspoon, non-stick saucepan, wooden spoon, knife, plate

INGREDIENTS

for each person

2 eggs
2 teaspoons water
pinch of salt and a sprinkle of pepper
knob of butter
slices of bread

METHOD

1. Make a piece of toast for each person and keep it warm.
2. Beat the eggs and water in a small bowl together with the salt and pepper.
3. Melt the butter, in a non-stick saucepan if possible, then turn down the heat.
4. Pour in the egg mixture and stir gently with a wooden spoon until the eggs are just beginning to set.
5. Remove from heat — the eggs carry on scrambling themselves for a little while after you have finished cooking them.
6. Butter the toast and serve the scrambled eggs piled up on it.

Fried Eggs

EQUIPMENT

cup, frying pan, tablespoon, slice, plate, knife

INGREDIENTS

for each person

1 egg

a little oil

METHOD

1. Heat the oil in a frying pan, then very carefully put in the eggs. Do this one at a time, by first breaking the egg into a cup and then pouring it gently into the pan.
2. Sizzle gently, carefully spooning the oil over the top of the eggs to seal the yolks. When the whites are firm, the eggs are cooked. Remove from the pan with a slice.
3. Serve on buttered toast, fried bread, or with grilled bacon and sausages.

Bacon and Banana Sandwiches

EQUIPMENT

frying pan, kitchen paper, knife, chopping board, plate

INGREDIENTS

to serve 1

2 slices brown bread and butter

1 banana

2 slices bacon, back or streaky

METHOD

1. Cook the bacon slices in a frying pan, using no extra fat, over medium heat until crisp.
2. Remove them from the pan and blot with kitchen paper.
3. Arrange them on one slice of bread.
4. Slice the banana and put it on the bacon, then put the other piece of bread on top.

Packed Lunch

These are a few ideas for packed lunch. Make your own for school and give the rest of the family ideas for a snack lunch at work. Some of these are in edible containers. The fillings are suggestions to start you thinking up your own combinations. Use your favourite sauces, pickles, or dressings like mayonnaise, to make the contents more interesting.

ROLLERS

Use crusty rolls as edible packaging for your lunch.

METHOD

1. Cut the top off the roll.
2. Pull out nearly all the soft inside.
3. Stuff the shell with a filling you have chosen and replace the top.

Two filling ideas coming up — but try your own special mixtures as well.

TUNA FISH AND TOMATO

EQUIPMENT

tin opener, tablespoon, fork, knife, bowl

INGREDIENTS

enough for two Rollers

99g	tin of tuna fish	3½oz
1	tomato	1
	salt and pepper	

METHOD

1. Open the tin of tuna and spoon it into a bowl. Mash it carefully with a fork.
2. Cut the tomato into small pieces.
3. Mix the tomato and tuna together in a bowl and add salt and pepper to your liking.

CHICKEN, CELERY AND PEANUTS

EQUIPMENT

sharp knife, chopping board, fork, small bowl, tablespoon

INGREDIENTS

2 tablespoons leftover chicken meat
2 sticks celery
1 tablespoon mayonnaise
1 tablespoon peanuts
salt and pepper

METHOD

1. Chop up the chicken into 1cm (½ inch) chunks.
2. Slice the celery into 1cm (½ inch) pieces.
3. Mix chicken and celery together in a bowl and stir in the mayonnaise.
4. Add the peanuts, then salt and pepper to your taste.

PITTA PACKS

White or wholemeal Pitta bread is oval shaped, flat and hollow. Cut each piece in half and you have a ready made pocket to pack with your favourite lunch filling.

EQUIPMENT

knife, bowl, chopping board, spoon

Three ideas for FILLINGS
enough for 1 person.

Use your imagination to invent more of your own.

1. Cold sliced sausages and cucumber chunks.
2. Chopped hard boiled egg mixed with 2 teaspoons of mayonnaise and a chopped spring onion.
3. Shredded lettuce with a sliced tomato and a tablespoon of grated cheese.

COLD TUB LUNCHES

Use an empty margarine tub as a container and fill it with a complete cold meal. The best tubs have sturdy sides and firm, snap on lids.

EQUIPMENT

knife, tablespoon, cup, chopping board

enough for one person

1. Two cold cooked fish fingers and 2 tablespoons coleslaw.

2. Two tablespoons of cottage cheese, one apple (cored but not peeled) cut into four, then sliced, 4 walnut halves.

3. Chicken Salad

INGREDIENTS

2	lettuce leaves	2
2 slices	chicken meat	2 slices
1	tomato cut into four	1
2cm	cucumber cut into chunks	1 inch

DRESSING

1 teaspoon lemon juice
4 teaspoons salad oil
salt and pepper

METHOD

1. Wash and dry the lettuce leaves clean and place in the bottom of the tub.
2. Arrange the chicken meat, tomato and cucumber prettily.
3. Mix the dressing ingredients together in a cup, then pour over the salad.
4. Snap the lid on tightly.

Everyone rushes in from school or work starving. Here are some satisfying snacks for two to fend off the hunger pangs. Make half portions if you'll be eating supper later.

Luigi's Pasta Bows

Luigi likes his pasta with a fishy sauce.

EQUIPMENT

saucepans (one for pasta, one for sauce), wooden spoon, colander, ovenproof dish, scales, measuring jug

INGREDIENTS

50g	pasta bows	2oz
25g	butter	1oz
25g	flour	1oz
275ml	milk	½ pint
99g	can tuna fish	3½oz
50g	grated cheddar cheese	2oz
	sprig of parsley (optional garnish)	
	salt and pepper	

METHOD

1. Cook the pasta as directed on the packet.
2. Make the sauce while the pasta is cooking. Melt the butter in a saucepan over low heat, stir in the flour and cook gently for one minute.
3. Remove from heat and gradually stir in the milk, adding a little at a time and making sure there are no lumps. Add a dash of salt and sprinkle of pepper.
4. Return to the heat and bring to the boil, stirring all the time till the sauce thickens, then take it off the heat.
5. When the pasta is cooked, drain it well in a colander, then put it back in the saucepan. Add the sauce and the tuna with the oil drained off. Stir in gently so you don't break up the fish too much.
6. Tip the mixture into a buttered ovenproof dish, then sprinkle the cheese on the top. Place the dish under a hot grill for a minute or two till the cheese has melted and browned.
7. Just before serving, put the sprig of parsley on top to make it look pretty.

Cornish Doorsteps

Anchovies on this version of cheese on toast make a really special combination.

EQUIPMENT

bread knife, board, grater, knife, scales

INGREDIENTS

2 slices	crusty bread	2 slices
50g	grated cheddar cheese	2oz
4	anchovy fillets	4

METHOD

1. Toast the bread on one side.
2. Divide the cheese between the slices and spread it evenly over the uncooked sides of the bread.
3. Lay the anchovies across the top.
4. Place under a hot grill till the cheese is melted and bubbling.

Pancakes

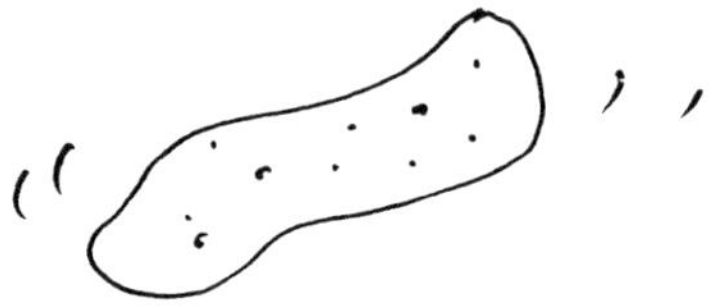

Usually served with lemon and sugar as in this recipe.

EQUIPMENT

Sieve, mixing bowl, wooden spoon, cup, small frying pan, tablespoon, palette knife, plate for keeping pancakes warm, serving plate

INGREDIENTS

100g	plain flour	4oz
250ml	milk	½ pint
1	egg	1
	pinch of salt	
	oil for frying	
	lemon juice	
	sugar	

METHOD

1. Sift the flour and salt together in a mixing bowl, then make a hollow in the middle with a wooden spoon. Break the egg into a cup, then pour it into the dent.
2. Gradually beat the flour into the egg using the wooden spoon, adding a little milk as you go along to give you a thick creamy mixture. Carry on beating till all the flour is mixed in and there are no lumps. Stir in the rest of the milk.
3. Heat a tablespoon of oil in a 17cm (7 inch) frying pan over medium heat and swirl it around to coat the base. When it's hot, spoon in enough batter to cover the bottom of the pan thinly. 2 — 3 tablespoons will be just about right for a pan this size and this mixture should make about 8 pancakes. A larger pan will need more tablespoons of batter to coat the base and will make less pancakes.
4. When the batter has set and the pancake is browned underneath (peep by lifting up the edge with a palette knife) turn it over with the palette knife or a fish slice and brown the other side. DON'T try tossing it unless you've already been taught how to do it or you don't mind eating pancakes off the floor!
5. Put it on a plate and keep warm.
6. Make the rest of the batter into pancakes and add to the pile on the plate.
7. Sprinkle each one with lemon juice and sugar.
Roll up and arrange on a serving plate.

Poor Boys

Fancy something sweet? Try these, they are delicious.

EQUIPMENT

Bread knife, board, fork, shallow dish, frying pan, palette knife, knife, scales, plate, tablespoon (tblsp), bowl

INGREDIENTS

4 slices	stale brown bread	4 slices
2	eggs	2
3tblsp	milk	3tblsp
50g	butter	2oz
dash	salt	dash
	Apricot jam, syrup or honey	

METHOD

1. Cut the crusts off the bread.
2. Beat the eggs in a bowl with a fork till frothy, add the milk and salt and beat again. Pour into a shallow dish.
3. Dip one piece of bread in the mixture, then turn it over so that both sides are coated.
4. Melt 12g (½oz) butter in a small frying pan over medium heat.
5. When the butter is bubbling in the pan, put the slice of bread in. Cook till the underneath is brown (check by lifting up a corner with a palette knife and peeping).
6. Turn the slice over and brown the other side.
7. Keep warm while you cook the other slices of bread. Add a little more butter to the frying pan each time.
8. Serve spread with jam, syrup or honey.

Croque Monsieur

Crunchy fried bread sandwich idea from France filled with oozy cheese and ham.

EQUIPMENT

Knife, grater, frying pan, fish slice, plate

INGREDIENTS

enough for 2

4 slices	buttered bread	4 slices
50g	grated cheddar cheese	2oz
2 slices	ham	2 slices
	butter *or* margarine for frying	

METHOD

1. Cover two slices of bread with cheese on the buttered side, then put a slice of ham on each one too.
2. Put the other slices of bread on the top of the ham, buttered side on the inside, to make two sandwiches.
3. Melt a walnut sized lump of butter or margarine in a frying pan over medium heat. Put the sandwich in and fry till golden brown underneath.
4. Very carefully turn the sandwich over with a fish slice and cook the other side. Put on a plate and keep warm.
5. Cook the other sandwich, adding another walnut of butter or margarine if necessary.

Emergency Supper

For days when the adults are eating late, going out to eat or just busy, and you're ready to eat now.

Egg and Bacon Spaghetti

Sounds like breakfast in Italy, but it's a yummy, fast and filling meal any time of the day.

EQUIPMENT

Saucepan, cup, fork, tablespoon (tblsp), small frying pan, colander, fish slice, plate for keeping bacon warm, knife, chopping board, serving plate, scales, grater

INGREDIENTS

enough for 1, multiply the ingredients for more people

50g	spaghetti	2oz
1	egg	1
1tblsp	milk	1tblsp
2 rashers	bacon, back or streaky	2 rashers
25g	butter	1oz
	salt and pepper	
	grated parmesan or cheddar cheese	

METHOD

1. Chop the bacon into the frying pan, then fry (using no extra fat) till the bacon is crispy. Remove from the pan with a fish slice, put on a plate and keep warm.
2. Cook the spaghetti in a saucepan of boiling salted water for 10 minutes. Drain off the water using a colander, then put the spaghetti back into the saucepan and stir in the butter.
3. Break the egg into a cup and add the milk. Beat them together with a fork. Add a little salt and pepper. Pour this mixture over the hot spaghetti and stir round well. The egg scrambles itself on to the spaghetti strands.
4. Scatter over the crispy bacon.
5. Turn out on to a plate and eat with grated parmesan or cheddar.

Gold Rush Beans

A fast and tasty beanpot for two people

EQUIPMENT

sharp knife, tablespoon (tblsp), draining spoon, teaspoon (teasp), saucers, tin opener, ovenproof dish, chopping board, frying pan

INGREDIENTS

2 thick slices	lean ham	2 thick slices
1tblsp	oil	1tblsp
1 small	onion	1 small
1 450g	can baked beans	15.9oz
1teasp	brown sugar	1teasp
1 heaped teasp	tomato puree	1 heaped teasp
1teasp	Worcestershire sauce	1teasp
1teasp	made mustard	1teasp

METHOD

1. Heat the oven to Gas Mark 4, (350°F, 180°C).
2. Peel and chop the onion and fry in the oil gently over low heat till softened. Remove from the frying pan with a draining spoon and keep in a saucer on one side.
3. Cut the ham into small cubes about this big  and fry gently till browned. Remove with a draining spoon and put in a separate saucer from the onion.
4. Open the can of beans and empty the contents into an ovenproof dish. Add the brown sugar, tomato puree, mustard and Worcestershire sauce. Stir well.
5. Sprinkle the fried onions over and stir through. Put the pot in the oven and cook for ¾ hour.
6. Scatter the ham cubes on the top just before serving.

PIZZA MARIA

A long recipe, but a quick supper dish. **Serves 2**

EQUIPMENT

teaspoon (teasp), tablespoon (tblsp), large bowl, small saucepan, small frying pan, sharp knife, fish slice, chopping board, tin opener, grater, sieve, clingfilm, garlic squeezer, fork, rolling pin, scales, serving plate

INGREDIENTS

For the base

100g	plain flour	4oz
½teasp	baking powder	½teasp
	pinch of salt	
50g	butter or margarine	2oz
1tblsp	water	1tblsp
2	tablespoons oil	2

For the sauce

25g	butter or margarine	1oz
1 small	onion	1 small
2 cloves	garlic	2 cloves
210g	can tomatoes	7½oz
1tblsp	tomato puree	1tblsp
1teasp	basil	1teasp
	salt and pepper	

For the topping

Choose one of these (plus 50g (2oz) grated cheddar)

1. 3 thin slices salami.
2. 1 chopped slice of ham and a sliced tomato.
3. 2 canned sardines.

METHOD

Base

1. Sift the flour and baking powder together into a large bowl and add the salt.
2. Rub the butter or margarine into the mixture till it looks like crumbs.
3. Add the water, then, using your fingers, gather everything in the bowl together so you have a stiffish dough. Knead lightly into a smooth ball, then wrap in clingfilm and leave to chill in the fridge while you make the sauce.

Sauce

1. Melt the butter or margarine in a small pan over gentle heat.
2. Peel and chop the onion and peel and crush the garlic, then fry them gently for 2 — 3 minutes till softened.
3. Open the can of tomatoes, drain them and add to the pan, mashing them down.
4. Add the tomato puree, basil, salt and pepper and cook for about 4—5 minutes (or longer) till the mixture has thickened.

To assemble the Pizza

take the dough out of the fridge

1. Shape it into a round, then on a floured surface with a floured rolling pin, roll out to 0.5cm (¼ inch) thick.
2. Heat the oil in a small frying pan and fry the dough till brown underneath and puffed up on top. Turn over.
3. While the other side is cooking slowly, spread the sauce over the cooked side, then arrange the topping of your choice over this. Sprinkle cheese over everything, plus extra pepper if you like it.
4. Place under a hot grill till the cheese bubbles.

Chunky Chicken Pie

Persuade your mum to keep a can of Chunky Chicken in the larder and a packet of frozen puff pastry in the freezer and you can knock up this super supper in no time. Remember to defrost the puff pastry first (or use the Hot Hands Pastry recipe on p. 20)

EQUIPMENT

tin opener, pie plate, rolling pin, pastry brush, teaspoon, sharp knife, cup, fork

INGREDIENTS
to serve 2

484g	can Chunky Chicken	16oz
210g	packet frozen puff pastry	7½oz
1	egg	1
	water	
	flour	

METHOD

1. Heat the oven to Gas Mark 6 (400°F, 200°C)
2. Open the can of Chunky Chicken and empty its contents into a pie plate.
3. Roll out the pastry on a floured work top with a floured rolling pin to slightly larger than the pie plate. Wet the rim of the plate with water, then place the pastry loosely on the top. Press down round the edge so that the pastry sticks to the rim of the plate. Trim the edges with a sharp knife, and make a pattern with a fork.
4. Gather up the scraps and roll out again. Cut into shapes to decorate the top. Stick into position with water.
5. Beat the egg in a cup with 2 teaspoons of water, then brush all over the top with a pastry brush to glaze.
6. Put in the oven and bake for 25 minutes till the pastry is risen, crispy and golden.

FOOD FOR WEEKENDS AND HOLIDAYS

All recipes serve four

SOUP

Tomato and Orange Soup with Croutons

A pretty orange soup with a delicate flavour. It's best made with fresh tomatoes, so try it in the summer when they are cheap.

EQUIPMENT

Bread knife, chopping board, sharp knife, draining spoon, 2 saucepans, frying pan, measuring jug, scales, tablespoon (tblsp), teaspoon (teasp), sieve

INGREDIENTS

500g	tomatoes	1lb
1tblsp	oil	1tblsp
1 small	onion	1 small
1 pinch	dried oregano	1 pinch
1teasp	Worcestershire sauce	1teasp
150ml	orange juice	¼ pint
	salt and white pepper	
575ml	chicken stock	1 pint

METHOD

1. Peel and chop the onion. Heat the oil in a saucepan, then gently fry the onion till soft but not brown.
2. Coarsely chop the tomatoes and add to the pan with the oregano, chicken stock (made from a cube) and Worcestershire sauce. Bring to the boil, then turn down and simmer for 15 minutes.
3. Remove from the heat. Strain the mixture through a sieve into a clean saucepan, pushing hard with the back of a spoon to squeeze all the juice through.
4. Add the orange juice, and salt and pepper to taste, then re-heat.

Serve with **Croutons**.

Croutons

These are small cubes of fried bread to sprinkle on soup as a garnish.

INGREDIENTS

4 slices	brown bread	4 slices
1	garlic clove (optional)	1
50g	butter	2oz

METHOD

1. Cut the crusts off the bread, then cut the bread into 1cm (½ inch) cubes.
2. Peel then slice the clove of garlic. Melt the butter in a frying pan. Fry the garlic for about 30 seconds, then take it out and throw away. This just flavours the butter slightly.
3. Fry the bread cubes till golden on all sides. Remove with a draining spoon and blot on kitchen paper.

GREEN PEA SOUP

This is bright Kermit green and delicious.
You make it in the blender so ask permission first.

EQUIPMENT

measuring jug, teaspoon (teasp), tablespoon (tblsp), saucepan, blender, serving bowl

INGREDIENTS

900g	frozen peas	2lbs
575ml	chicken stock	1 pint
2teasp	lemon juice	2teasp
	salt and pepper	
1tblsp	single cream (if you have some)	1tblsp

METHOD

1. Put the frozen peas in a saucepan and add half the chicken stock (made from a cube). Bring to the boil, then turn down the heat and simmer for 10 minutes.
2. Remove from the heat, carefully pour into the blender and whizz to a puree. Return to the saucepan.
3. Add the rest of the stock, lemon juice and salt and pepper to taste.
4. Re-heat, pour into a serving bowl and, just before serving, swirl the cream over the top.

STARTERS

FAT CAT PATE

Easy as winking, this is a smoked mackerel pâté everyone will ask you to make again. You'll need permission to use the blender.

EQUIPMENT

Blender, tablespoon (tblsp), fork, teaspoon (teasp), sharp knife, scales

INGREDIENTS

225g	smoked mackerel fillet	8oz
100g	cream cheese	4oz
1 teasp	Dijon mustard	1teasp
1tblsp	lemon juice	1tblsp
	salt and black pepper	
	lemon quarters	
	or	
	black olives for decoration (if you have them)	

METHOD

1. Peel the skin from the smoked mackerel fillet.
2. Put mackerel, cream cheese, mustard, lemon juice, a pinch of salt and three shakes of black pepper into the liquidiser and blend till almost smooth — it's quite a good idea not to make it too smooth so you get an interesting texture.
3. Pack into a serving bowl — it looks good in an earthenware one — and rough up the top with a fork. Put an olive or two on the top if you have some, or serve with lemon quarters and a pile of **Melba Toast.**

Melba Toast

Crunchy extra thin toast triangles.

EQUIPMENT

Serrated edged knife, breadboard

INGREDIENTS

4 pieces white sliced bread

METHOD

1. Cut the crusts from the bread, then carefully toast the slices on both sides.
2. While the toast is still warm and using a serrated edged knife (being very careful not to cut yourself) gently saw through the toasted slices horizontally so you are left with two very thin pieces with one side toasted and the other side not. Cut each thin piece in half again to give you triangles.

3. Place the triangles browned side down under the grill and briefly toast the uncooked sides so the triangles curl up.

MELON BALLS IN CURRY CREAM

This is a good excuse to have a go with a melon baller if you have one. If you haven't, cut the melon into cubes.

EQUIPMENT

Chopping board, sharp knife, tablespoon, teaspoon (teasp), melon baller, whisk, bowls, serving dish

INGREDIENTS

1	ripe melon	1
150ml	double cream	¼pint
½teasp	medium curry paste	½teasp
1teasp	lemon juice	1teasp
1	lettuce	1
	few sliced almonds for garnish	

METHOD

1. Cut the melon in half and scoop out the seeds. (NOTE: if you wash and dry them, then thread them sideways on to cotton you'll have a terrific string of beads — but do it when you've finished cooking).
2. Using a melon baller cut out as many spheres or half spheres as you can from the melon flesh and place them in a bowl. Or cut the melon flesh into cubes.

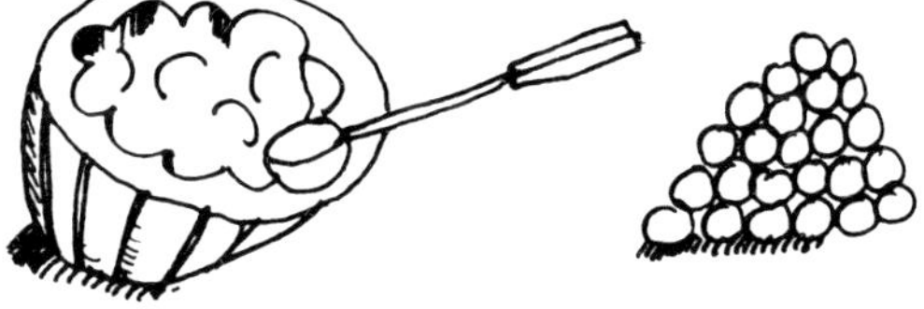

3. Using a whisk, beat the cream in a bowl until thick, but not stiff and stir in the curry paste and lemon juice.
4. Stir this mixture into the bowl of melon balls or cubes, then leave to chill in the fridge.
5. Wipe or wash and dry the lettuce clean and fan the leaves out on a serving dish.
6. Pile the melon mixture into the middle of the lettuce and sprinkle sliced almonds on top for garnish.

MAIN COURSES

Homemade Quarter Pounders

The best beefburgers really are homemade ones.

EQUIPMENT

bowl, teaspoon, knife, grater, frying pan, slice, serving plate

INGREDIENTS

500g	best minced beef	1lb

(best mince looks very red — the more pink the colour, the more fat is minced in as well and the more your beefburgers will shrink when the fat melts off in cooking).

pinch of dried herbs

4 teaspoons grated onion

salt

lots of fresh ground pepper if you have a grinder, otherwise about 4 good shakes out of the pepperpot

4 sesame seed baps

oil

flour

METHOD

1. Mix the first five ingredients together in a bowl, then divide the mixture into four.
2. Sprinkle a worktop with flour, then put a quarter of the mixture on it, shaping it into a flat round with your hands. Do the same with the other three portions of the mixture.
3. Heat a little oil in a frying pan. Put the beefburgers in and cook them over a medium heat till brown underneath.
4. Turn over with a slice and cook the other sides.
5. Split the baps with a knife and put one beefburger in each. Serve with a choice of:

Tomato ketchup
lettuce
onion rings
relishes
mayonnaise
slices of gherkin

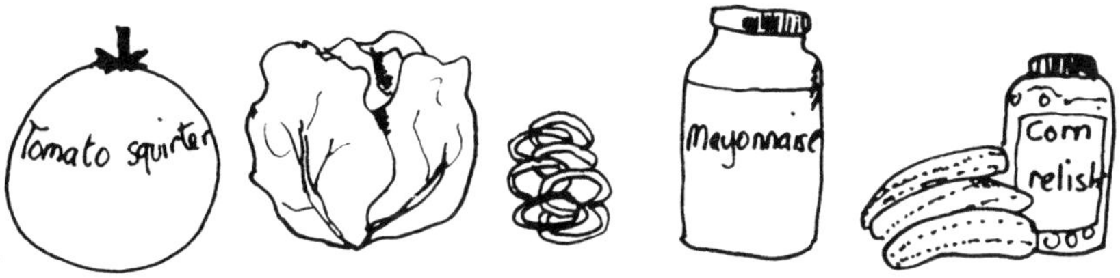

For **CHEESEBURGERS** put a slice of cheese on the freshly cooked beefburger before you put it in the bap. The heat of the meat will begin to melt the cheese.

Beef with Mushrooms

A dark and interesting stew which fills the kitchen with the most delectable aroma while it's cooking.

EQUIPMENT

sharp knife, tablespoon (tblsp), J-cloth or kitchen paper, bowl, frying pan, casserole, scales, measuring jug, chopping board, teaspoon, draining spoon

INGREDIENTS

700g	braising steak	1½lbs
1	medium onion	1
4tblsp	oil	4tblsp
50g	flour	2oz
	pinch dried thyme	
	or sprig fresh thyme	
100g	button mushrooms	4oz
575ml	beef stock	1pint
	salt and pepper	

METHOD

1. Peel and slice the onion. Wash and blot the mushrooms dry with a clean J-cloth or kitchen paper — don't peel them. Trim the fat from the meat, and cut it into bite-sized chunks.
2. Fry the onion slices in the oil in a medium sized frying pan till golden brown. Transfer to a casserole dish with a draining spoon.
3. Put the flour into a bowl and shake ½ teaspoon of salt and pepper into it. Mix well. Dip the meat chunks into this mixture so that they are well coated. Fry in the oil until browned all over.
4. Add the meat to the onions in the casserole. Then add the wiped mushrooms, cut into quarters if they're a bit too big.
5. Add the rest of the flour to the juice in the frying pan, then stir in the stock. Heat till thickened.
6. Pour over the contents of the casserole. Add the thyme. Put the lid on the casserole and cook at Gas Mark 4 (350°F, 180°C) for about 1½—2 hours till the meat is tender. Test by poking a piece with a knife to see if it's soft. Add extra salt and pepper to the gravy if you like.

Chicken in the Pot

This is so amazingly simple, even non-cooking adults can throw it together — they may need a little supervision though, so don't encourage them to start unless you are prepared to keep your eye on them.

EQUIPMENT

scales, potato peeler, tin opener, teaspoon (teasp), sharp knife, chopping board, large flameproof casserole with a lid

INGREDIENTS

approx 1kg	1 chicken	approx 2¼lbs
500g	potatoes	1lb
425g	can tomatoes	14oz
225g	packet frozen whole green beans	8oz
½teasp	dried mixed herbs	½teasp
	salt and pepper	

You need a flameproof casserole (which *can* be used on a hob) with a well fitting lid for this dish. If you use a frozen chicken *make sure* it's thoroughly defrosted, the giblets are removed, and the cavity inside is not still icy.

METHOD

1. Put the whole chicken into the flameproof casserole.
2. Peel and thickly slice the potatoes. Put into the pan around the chicken.
3. Open the can of tomatoes and tip the contents into the casserole with the herbs and 3 good pinches of salt and 4 good shakes of pepper. Put the lid on and cook everything over low heat for an hour or till the chicken is cooked. Test for tenderness by prodding with a knife.
4. Remove the lid and put the beans in the casserole. Cook for 15 minutes more.

Note — you can use other vegetables as well as, or instead of beans. Put root vegetables in when the potatoes are added and green vegetables when the beans go in.

Lizard Pie

Not really made from lizards, this is a flaky pastry pie with a filling based on pilchards — which are caught off the coast of Cornwall, near the Lizard. You can serve it hot or cold.

EQUIPMENT

scales, sharp knife, chopping board, frying pan, medium saucepan, tablespoon (tblsp), teaspoon (teasp), rolling pin, cup, pastry brush, serving plate, colander, slice, clean teacloth, fork

INGREDIENTS

100g	long grain rice	4oz
425g	can pilchards in tomato sauce	15oz
4	hard boiled eggs	4
1tblsp	finely chopped onion	1tblsp
25g	butter *or* margarine	1oz
1teasp	dried dill	1teasp
	or dried parsley	
	or	
1tblsp	chopped fresh parsley	1tblsp
	salt and pepper	
210g	packet frozen puff pastry (defrosted)	7½oz
1	egg	1

METHOD

1. Cook the rice in boiling salted water for exactly 12 minutes. Remove from the heat, and drain off the water with a colander. Put the rice back into the saucepan and pack a clean tea towel gently into the pan on top of the rice, then leave alone for the steam to finish off cooking the rice and keep it hot. This is the best way to cook rice — you can be sure of tender, separate grains.
2. Very gently fry the onion in the melted butter or margarine in a frying pan till soft. Add to the cooked rice.

3. Open the pilchard can and take out the fish. Discard the skin, the bones and the innards — only for artistic purposes, it's all quite edible. Flake the fish into chunks and add to the rice and onions. Stir in the tomato sauce from the can as well.
4. Add the dill or parsley, a half teaspoon of salt and 5 good shakes of pepper.
6. Roll the pastry into an oblong about ½cm (¼inch) thick. Pile the filling onto the middle of the pastry. Cut the eggs into quarters and poke into the filling. Moisten the edges of the pastry with water, then fold the long sides to the middle and seal them together — like a parcel. Press together the short ends and make doubly sure they are sealed by squidging the edges together with the prongs of a fork.
7. Put the pie on a baking sheet with the join underneath.
8. Brush the top of the pie with beaten egg mixed with a little water.
9. Cook at Gas Mark 7, (425°F 220°C) for 25 — 30 minutes till the pastry is risen, puffy and golden crisp. Transfer to a serving plate with a slice, or on to a wire rack to cool down.

DESSERTS

Chocolate and Orange Mousse

EQUIPMENT

3 basins, saucepan, fork, tablespoon (tblsp), serving dishes, whisk, piping bag, rosette nozzle, scales

INGREDIENTS

175g	plain chocolate	6oz
2	eggs	2
1tblsp	orange juice from a carton	1tblsp
150ml	double cream	¼pint

METHOD

1. Break the chocolate into squares and put in a basin. Place this basin over a small saucepan of simmering water till the chocolate has melted.
2. Separate the yolks from the whites of the eggs into two basins. Beat the yolks with the orange juice and add to the melted chocolate.
3. Whip half the cream thick and stir it thoroughly into the chocolate and orange mixture.
4. Beat the egg whites stiff and carefully fold them in too. Pour into four individual pots or a deep dish and leave to set in the fridge.
5. Whisk the rest of the cream stiff. Fill a piping bag and pipe rosettes of cream round the edge of the mousse for decoration.

Fresh Fruit Salad

This recipe involves a bit of fiddling about to prepare the fruit, but it's worth the trouble. You can use what fruit you like, these are just suggestions. You'll need to use a sharp knife so TAKE CARE.

EQUIPMENT

sharp knife, bowl, serrated edged knife, chopping board, teaspoon, tablespoon

INGREDIENTS

1 apple
2 bananas
1 orange
1 pear
small bunch of grapes
1 kiwi fruit
4 teaspoons lemon juice
4 tablespoons orange juice

METHOD

1. Wipe the apple, then cut into quarters. Remove the core and slice the rest thinly. Put in a serving bowl and sprinkle with a few drops of lemon juice. This stops the apple from going brown.
2. Peel the orange with a serrated knife, being sure to remove all the white pith. Cut the orange across into thin slices. Add to the bowl.
3. Cut each grape in half and remove the pips with the point of a knife. Add to the bowl.
4. Wipe the pear, core it and cut into slices. Sprinkle with lemon juice and add to the bowl.
5. Peel the bananas and slice across into rounds. Sprinkle lemon juice on the slices, then add to the rest of the fruit.
6. Thinly peel the kiwi fruit and cut it crossways into fine slices. Add to the bowl.
7. When all the fruit is in the serving bowl, pour over the orange juice.

Baked Alaska

A gasp-making pud. Just produce it nonchalantly and no one will guess how easy it is to make.

EQUIPMENT

tablespoon (tblsp), ovenproof dish, palette knife, whisk, knife, oven mitt

INGREDIENTS

1	sponge cake	1
1tblsp	black cherry	1tblsp
	or	
	other strong flavoured jam	
500ml	block vanilla ice cream	1pint
	taken straight from the freezer. You can use your own favourite flavour but vanilla is specially good in this recipe.	
3	egg whites	3
6tblsp	caster sugar	6tblsp

METHOD

1. Turn the oven on at Gas Mark 8, (450°F 230°C) to heat while you assemble the Baked Alaska.
2. Trim the sponge cake base so that when the ice cream block is put on top, a 1cm (½ inch) rim of cake will show round the edge of the ice cream. Immediately put the ice cream back in the freezer till you need it again.
3. Place the sponge on a shallow ovenproof dish. Spread the jam on the sponge.
4. To make the meringue topping, whip the egg whites till very stiff, then fold in the sugar with a tablespoon.
5. Put the straight-from-the-freezer ice cream on to the sponge. Cover it quickly and completely with the meringue mixture using a palette knife and making ABSOLUTELY SURE there are no holes or gaps for the heat to get inside, Otherwise . . . disaster! Peak the outside up with a knife.
6. Put into the VERY HOT oven for 3 minutes — till the meringue peaks are just turning brown.
7. Take out of the oven using an oven mitt or cloth.
8. Eat immediately.

FOOD FOR PARTIES AND FETES

PARTIES

All recipes serve 8

Celery, Apple and Peanut Dip with Carrot and Cucumber Sticks or Crisps

A creamy dip with crunchy bits for scooping up with raw sticks of vegetables or crisps.

EQUIPMENT

basin, knife, spoon, chopping board, scales, tablespoon (tblsp), tray, bowl, fork, rolling pin, small plastic bag

INGREDIENTS

225g	cream *or* curd cheese	8oz
2 sticks	celery	2 sticks
1	red apple	1
50g	chopped *or* crushed salted peanuts	2oz
2tblsp	milk	2tblsp
	carrots, cucumber and/or crisps	

METHOD

1. Put the cream cheese in a basin and beat it smooth, gradually adding the milk. You can add a few drops of lemon juice after stirring in the milk to give a sharper flavour.
2. Wash, dry and finely chop the celery sticks. Add to the cheese.
3. Wipe, quarter, core and chop the apple. Add to the cheese.
4. Chop or crush the peanuts. To crush, place them in a small plastic bag and roll firmly with a rolling pin. Add to the cheese. The dip should be stiff enough not to drip on people's shoes, but not so stiff it breaks the vegetable sticks when you scoop it. Add a little extra milk if you think it needs it.
5. Put the dip in a pot on a tray and place sticks of washed and scrubbed carrot, and cucumber sticks around the pot to dunk with. Leave the skin on the cucumber. Crisps make good dippers too.

Spicy Chicken Drumsticks

Drumsticks with an interesting crunchy crust on the outside.

EQUIPMENT

tablespoon (tblsp), pastry brush, teaspoon (teasp), baking sheet, shallow dish, fork, serving plate, saucer

INGREDIENTS

8	chicken drumsticks	8
	watercress *or* mustard and cress for garnish	
	a little oil	
2tblsp	grated parmesan cheese	2tblsp
1tblsp	medium curry powder	1tblsp
1teasp	paprika	1teasp
1teasp	salt	1teasp

METHOD

1. Put the last four ingredients in a shallow dish and mix well with a fork.
2. Pour a little oil into a saucer then, using a pastry brush, paint the drumsticks with oil and dip them one by one into the mixture, making sure they are well coated.
3. Arrange in a baking tin and cook at Gas Mark 5 (375°F 190°C) for about ¾ hour till they are cooked through and crispy on the outside.
4. Arrange on a plate.
5. Put sprigs of watercress or mustard and cress around the edge for decoration.

STUFFED EGGS

Very appetising prettily arranged on lettuce leaves.

EQUIPMENT

knife, small bowl, teaspoon, fork, tin opener, tablespoon (tblsp), serving plate

INGREDIENTS

8	hard boiled eggs	8
2tblsp	mayonnaise	2tblsp
99g	can of tuna *or* sardines in tomato sauce	3½oz
2	anchovy fillets	2
	salt and pepper	
	lettuce leaves	

METHOD

1. Shell the eggs, cut them in half lengthways and scoop the yolks out into a bowl with a teaspoon. Mash them with a fork.
2. Open the sardine or tuna can and mash the contents into the yolks. Add the mayonnaise and salt and pepper to taste.
3. Spoon the mixture back into the egg whites, then decorate with thin strips of anchovy criss-crossed over the top.
4. Wash and dry the lettuce leaves clean, then arrange them on a serving plate. Put the stuffed egg halves on top, fanned out so they look like flower petals.

Hot Pups

These are miniature versions of the usual hot dogs, made with cocktail frankfurters.

EQUIPMENT

knife, saucepan, colander, serving plate, small bowls, tin opener

INGREDIENTS

8 baby bridge rolls

1 can cocktail frankfurters

butter

made mustard *or* tomato ketchup

METHOD

1. Split the rolls carefully down one side leaving the other side joined like a hinge. Butter both cut sides.
2. Heat the frankfurters according to the instructions on the can. Drain them.
3. Put a sausage in each roll.
4. Serve with small bowls of mustard and tomato ketchup for guests to help themselves.

Fruit Kebabs

Very pretty fruit-filled cocktail sticks. Use firm fruit so it is easy to spike on the stick. Make 3 or 4 for each person.

EQUIPMENT

tin opener, plates, knife, cocktail sticks, serving plate

INGREDIENTS

225g	can pineapple cubes	8oz
225g	can lychees	8oz
1 small	bunch black grapes	1 small

METHOD

1. Open the cans of pineapple and lychees and drain the contents. Cut the lychees in half.
2. Put the pineapple cubes, lychees and grapes on three plates.
3. Thread the cocktail sticks in the following order: pineapple cube, half a lychee, black grape.
4. Arrange them all on a pretty plate with the grape ends of the sticks pointing outwards to make a wheel pattern.

Quiche Lorraine

This is an open egg and bacon tart. Not everyone has the gift of perfect pastry making — you may have had experience in this direction yourself already, but if you use the Hot Hands Pastry recipe (p. 20) you can be pretty sure of success.

EQUIPMENT

rolling pin, 20cm (8") flan tin, frying pan, knife, grater, fork, scales, bowl, chopping board

INGREDIENTS

	Hot Hands Pastry (page 20)	
	flour for dusting the worktop	
4	rashers bacon, back *or* streaky	4
2	eggs	2
150ml	single cream *or* creamy milk	¼ pint
25g	grated cheddar	1oz
	salt and pepper	

METHOD

1. Preheat the oven to Gas Mark 6 (400°F 200°C).
2. Using a floured rolling pin and a floured worktop, roll out the pastry to fit inside a greased 20cm (8") flan tin.
3. Chop the bacon and fry it in a pan without extra fat till crispy.
4. Beat the eggs together with the cream or milk in a bowl.
Add a pinch of salt and two shakes of pepper.
5. Scatter the bacon over the base of the pastry and pour on the egg mixture. Sprinkle the cheese on top.
6. Put the quiche in the hot oven and bake for 35 minutes till risen, set, and brown on the top.

FETES

Flapjacks

Make lots of these or else you'll find there won't be many left when you arrive at the fête.

EQUIPMENT

bowl, fork, square baking tin, knife, slice, scales, plate

INGREDIENTS

100g	porridge oats	4oz
100g	softened butter *or* margarine	4oz
100g	soft dark brown sugar	4oz

METHOD

1. Heat the oven to Gas Mark 4 (350°F 180°C).
2. Put all the ingredients together in a bowl and mix well with a fork.
3. Press into a buttered 20cm (8") square tin.
4. Put the flapjacks in the oven and cook for 30 minutes till they darken to a golden brown.
5. Remove from the oven and mark into wide fingers with a knife, then leave to cool in the tin.
6. When completely cold remove with a slice breaking along the marked lines as you do.
7. Arrange on a plate.

Cheese Straws

These will keep in an airtight tin — but usually you'll find they're all eaten even before they've cooled down.

EQUIPMENT

rolling pin, knife, grater, baking sheet, pastry brush, slice, wire rack, scales, cup, fork

INGREDIENTS

210g	packet defrosted puff pastry	7½oz
100g	grated cheddar cheese	4oz
1	egg	1
	paprika pepper	
	French mustard	
	sesame seeds	

METHOD

1. Sprinkle some flour on a work top, then, using a floured rolling pin, roll out the pastry to an oblong about 0.5cm (¼") thick.
2. Spread the mustard thinly over one half of the pastry starting at one of the short edges. Sprinkle it with cheese. Fold the uncovered half over the top of the cheese so that it is trapped between the layers of pastry. Roll out again to 0.5cm (¼ inch) thick.
3. Cut the pastry into strips about 15cm (6") long and 1cm (½ inch) wide. Carefully lay them side by side on a greased baking sheet. Leave some straight and twist some like barley sugar. You can make one strip into a circle by sticking the ends together with water so it can be used as a pastry ring to hold the sticks together when they're cooked.
4. Beat an egg and a little water in a cup with a fork, then brush the tops of the sticks and ring with it, using a pastry brush. Sprinkle a little paprika on some, and sesame seeds on others.
5. Heat the oven to Gas Mark 8 (450°F 230°C). Put the cheese straws in to bake for 10 — 12 minutes till crispy and brown.
6. Remove carefully from the baking sheet using a slice, then cool on a wire rack.

NOTE: You can leave out the mustard if you don't like it.

Shortbread

This melt-in-the-mouth biscuit is very popular at fêtes.

EQUIPMENT

sieve, bowl, knife, shallow cake tin, scales, slice

INGREDIENTS

175g	plain flour	6oz
50g	caster sugar	2oz
100g	butter	4oz

METHOD

1. Sift the flour into a bowl with the sugar.
2. Cut the butter into pieces, then rub into flour and sugar gently till the mixture looks like breadcrumbs.
3. Gather together into a ball and knead very lightly on a floured worktop till the mixture is smooth.
4. Butter a 16cm (7 inch) shallow round cake tin and press the mixture in evenly with a fork or your fingers.
5. Mark into eight sections with a knife.
6. Heat the oven to Gas Mark 4 (350°F 180°C) and cook the shortbread for 30 minutes. Turn down the heat to Gas Mark 3 (325°F 160°C) and cook for 30 minutes more.
7. Remove from the oven and cut the section lines again. Leave to cool in the tin, then carefully prise the pieces out with a slice so you don't break them. Remember that shortbread is very brittle.

Homemade Bread

There's nothing quite so delicious as homemade bread. The more you knead it the better it is so you can get rid of all your frustrations while giving the dough a good punch. The quantities given are enough for two small loaves.

EQUIPMENT

small bowl, large bowl, sieve, tablespoon (tblsp), sharp knife, clingfilm, baking sheet, wire rack, scales, measuring jug, teaspoon (teasp)

INGREDIENTS

400g	wholemeal flour	1lb
200g	strong plain flour	8oz
2 level teasp	salt	2 level teasp
2 tblsp	oil	2tblsp
2 level teasp	dried yeast	2 level teasp
1 level teasp	sugar	1 level teasp
400ml	warm water	¾ pint
	sesame seeds, cracked wheat *or* oatmeal if you have some, to decorate the top.	

METHOD

1. Dissolve the sugar in a bowl of the warm water. Add the yeast granules and stir well, then leave for 10 — 15 minutes in a warm place till frothy.
2. Put the wholemeal flour in a large bowl, then sift in the strong white flour. Add the salt. Stir in the oil.
3. Pour in the yeast liquid and mix to a dough.
4. Sprinkle flour on your work top and tip the dough out on it. Knead vigorously till smooth.
5. Cut the dough in half and shape into two balls. Put them on an oiled baking sheet. Cover loosely with a piece of lightly oiled clingfilm, then leave in a warm place to rise to twice their original size. This will take at least an hour.
6. Pre-heat the oven to Gas Mark 7 (425°F 220°C).
7. Sprinkle the tops of the loaves with sesame seeds, cracked wheat or oatmeal.
8. Put the loaves into the oven and bake them for 40 minutes. Cool on a wire rack.

NOTE: For shiny loaves glaze the tops with beaten egg and water.

FOOD FOR OUTDOORS

Picnic Seaside Sports' day and Garden Food

MEAT AND TATER PASTIES

enough for 4

These are almost a whole meal in themselves and are a useful way to finish off leftover meat. All you need to go with them is a tomato or a crunchy green apple.

EQUIPMENT

knife, grater, saucer, rolling pin, pastry brush, bowl, cup, baking sheet, wire rack, scales, tablespoon (tblsp).

INGREDIENTS

210g	packet frozen puff pastry (defrosted)	7½oz
	or Hot Hands Pastry (see p. 20)	
225g	leftover meat	8oz
	or	
210g	can corned beef	7½oz
225g	cold boiled potatoes	8oz
1tblsp	grated onion	1tblsp
1tblsp	fresh chopped parsley	1tblsp
	dash Worcestershire sauce	
	salt and pepper	
1	egg	1

METHOD

1. Trim the leftover meat or open the can of corned beef and cut it into small cubes. Cut the potatoes into the same sized cubes. Put the meat and potato into a bowl.
2. Add the onion, parsley and Worcestershire sauce and mix together.
3. Dust the worktop with flour, then roll out the pastry to a square 0.5cm (¼ inch) thick. Cut out 4 circles using a saucer as a guide.
4. Pile ¼ of the meat mixture into the middle of each pastry circle. Brush the pastry edges with water, then bring the sides up to meet over the top of the filling. Crimp the edges together to make a curly edge.
5. Place the pasties on a greased baking sheet.
6. Beat the egg in a cup with a little water and brush the pasties with it.
7. Heat the oven to Gas Mark 7 (425°F 220°C). Put the pasties in and cook for 25 minutes till they are crisp and golden.
8. Take out of the oven and cool on a wire rack.

METROS

Monster French rolls stuffed with everything but the kitchen sink.

EQUIPMENT

sharp knife, chopping board, spoons and forks for measuring and mixing

INGREDIENTS

1 roll for each person

butter

METHOD

1. Cut the rolls in half and butter each half. Fill with one of the following — or your own particular favourite.
2. Sliced ham, lettuce, tomato slices.
3. Cold cooked sausage slices with sweet pickle.
4. Cream or cottage cheese with sliced apple and a few walnuts.
5. Tuna, drained, mixed with mayonnaise and with some cucumber slices tucked in too.
5. Cold scrambled egg with cold crispy bacon and some crunchy lettuce.
6. Grated cheddar with a bit of picallili and a few sprigs of watercress.

SALADS

Salads are very suitable for eating outdoors — you can transport them easily in plastic boxes — or even large size margarine tubs. Eat with plastic forks. Most salads need a dressing to make them moist or to keep all the ingredients together. Two very useful dressings which you can use for lots of other dishes as well are vinaigrette and mayonnaise (see pages 21 and 22). If there is lettuce in your salad, take the vinaigrette in a separate container and add it just before eating.

FRUITY COLESLAW

enough for 6

A truly delectable crunch dressed in mayonnaise. You can use bought mayonnaise or make your own.

EQUIPMENT

grater, bowl, strainer, tablespoon, sharp knife, chopping board, measuring jug, scales

INGREDIENTS

225g	white cabbage	½lb
100g	scrubbed carrots	¼lb
50g	peanuts	2oz
1 small	tin pineapple in its own juice	1 small
150ml	mayonnaise	¼ pint

METHOD

1. Grate the cabbage or cut it very thinly. Put in a bowl.
2. Grate the carrots on the coarse hole of the grater. Add to the bowl.
3. Drain the pineapple and add to the bowl. Discard the juice or drink it.
4. Add the mayonnaise to the bowl and mix well.
5. Stir in the peanuts.

TOMATO SALAD WITH FRESH HERBS

The fresh scent of the herbs makes this irresistible. The quantities given are enough for 6.

EQUIPMENT

sharp knife, bowl, tablespoon, chopping board

INGREDIENTS

700g	firm tomatoes	1½lbs
6	spring onions	6
	few sprigs parsley	
	few leaves of fresh basil	
	or	
	pinch of dried basil	
	vinaigrette dressing (see p. 22)	

METHOD

1. Wipe the tomatoes and cut them into thick slices. Place in a bowl.
2. Trim the spring onions, removing the roots and any brown leaves. Wash and dry them, then chop into 0.5cm (¼ inch) chunks including the green tops. Scatter over the tomatoes.
3. Finely chop the parsley and basil leaves (if using fresh) and sprinkle on top.
4. Spoon over the vinaigrette dressing.

FOOD FOR PRESENTS

Fresh Cream Chocolate Truffles

These taste like a dream and make the most wonderful present for a special friend or grown up. Find a little box and pack the truffles in it, then tie up with a piece of ribbon.

EQUIPMENT

2 small bowls, small saucepan, tablespoon (tblsp), sieve, teaspoon, scales

INGREDIENTS

175g	plain chocolate	6oz
75g	pre-softened unsalted butter	3oz
175g	sifted icing sugar	6oz
2tblsp	single cream	2tblsp
	sifted cocoa *or* chocolate vermicelli	

METHOD

1. Melt the chocolate in a bowl over a small saucepan of simmering water.
2. Take off the heat and cool for a couple of minutes, stir in the softened butter, then cream.
3. Sift the icing sugar into a bowl and add gradually to the chocolate mixture, stirring well.
4. Chill the mixture in the fridge for at least 2 hours.
5. When the mixture is stiff, take it out of the fridge and nip off small pieces with your finger and thumb, or scoop off teaspoonsful. Shape into balls, then roll the balls in some cocoa or chocolate vermicelli sprinkled generously on a worktop.
6. Chill again.
7. Pack up in pretty boxes or little china or pottery containers. Tie up with ribbons.

Butterscotch Stickjaw

Fantastic buttery toffee. Break into chunks and wrap up the pieces in crackly cellophane paper. This recipe involves boiling sugar so ask permission and don't do it unsupervised.

EQUIPMENT

heavy saucepan, tablespoon (tblsp), cup, swiss roll tin, knife, scales

INGREDIENTS

350g	brown sugar	12oz
60g	butter	2½oz
1tblsp	vinegar	1tblsp
2tblsp	boiling water	2tblsp
	oil	

METHOD

1. Oil a swiss roll tin.
2. Put all the ingredients together in a heavy bottomed saucepan and melt them over gentle heat till the sugar has dissolved and the mixture starts to boil. BOILING SUGAR IS VERY HOT INDEED. BE CAREFUL WITH THE NEXT FEW STEPS.
3. Turn the heat up and boil the mixture over medium heat until half a spoonful dropped in a cup of cold water sets brittle.
4. Pour carefully into the oiled swiss roll tin and allow to cool. Mark into squares with a knife before it sets solid.
5. When completely set tap into square pieces with the back of a knife and wrap up in cellophane.

Message Cake

A flat, thin cake for writing a message on. Choose your cake tin with the length of your message in mind.

EQUIPMENT

cake tin, 1 large bowl and 2 smaller bowls, sieve, electric beater, whisk or wooden spoon, tablespoons, wire rack, palette knife, teaspoon, piping bag and writing nozzle, special plate, scales

INGREDIENTS

for the cake

100g	SR flour	4oz
100g	caster sugar	4oz
100g	soft margarine	4oz
2	eggs	2

for the icing:

250g	sifted icing sugar	½lb
125g	pre-softened butter	4oz
	two food colours	

METHOD

1. Heat the oven to Gas Mark 4 (350°F 180°C).
2. Put the sugar, margarine, eggs and sifted flour into a bowl. Using an electric beater (ask permission), hand whisk, or wooden spoon — in which case you'll have to do a lot more hard work — beat everything together till well mixed and smooth.
3. Grease the inside of the tin you choose then spoon the mixture in.
4. Put the cake in the oven and cook for 20 — 25 minutes until it is risen, brown and firm to the touch.
5. Turn out of the tin and cool on a wire rack.
6. Meanwhile, make the icing. Sift the icing sugar into a bowl with the softened butter. Beat it carefully with a wooden spoon until the sugar is well mixed in. Take out about 3 tablespoons and put it into a separate bowl. Add a few drops of food colouring and stir in.

7. Add a couple of drops of the other colour to the rest of the icing in the first bowl and stir, making sure you use different spoons for each different colour.
8. When the cake is completely cold (if it's at all warm the icing will melt) spread the larger amount of icing all over the top and sides of the cake with a palette knife.
9. Put the cake into the fridge for 10 minutes so the icing firms up.
10. Spoon the other-coloured icing into a piping bag with a writing nozzle. Practise squiggles and letters on a clean plate a few times so you get the feel of the piping bag full of icing (you can always put the icing you've squeezed out back into the bag for re-use.) Now you're ready to write your message.
11. Take the cake out of the fridge and lightly mark where each word is to go with the point of a knife. Then — write away!
12. Put the cake on a special plate with a doily and give a surprise to a friend or one of the family.

Peanut Butter

Just about everybody's favourite. This is made in a blender so ask permission first.

EQUIPMENT

scales, tablespoon (tblsp), blender, screw top jar

INGREDIENTS

225g	salted peanuts	8oz
1½tblsp	vegetable oil	1½tblsp

METHOD

1. Put the ingredients into the blender and whizz it till the mixture is how you like your peanut butter — a bit rough and crunchy or completely smooth. It takes longer to make it smooth.
2. Pack into a screw top jar and keep in the fridge.

Lemon Curd

Some people think this must be the food of the gods. Whether or not this is true, it's sensational and makes a really welcome present.

EQUIPMENT

bowl, lemon squeezer, small saucepan, egg whisk, wooden spoon, jam jar, cover, rubber band, grease proof paper circle, label.

INGREDIENTS

enough to make ½kg (1lb):

200g	caster sugar	8oz
100g	butter	4oz
2	eggs	2
	juice of two lemons	

METHOD

1. Whisk the eggs frothy in an ovenproof bowl.
2. Melt the butter with the sugar in a saucepan over gentle heat. Add the lemon juice. Pour into the beaten eggs.
3. Put the bowl over a pan of simmering water and cook until the mixture thickens, stirring all the time. It's important not to let the mixture get too hot or it will curdle.
4. Cool completely, then pack into a very clean, freshly washed and dried jar.
5. Put a circle of greaseproof paper on the top, then a mob cap of pretty paper or material secured with a rubber band.
6. Write 'Lemon Curd' on a sticky label to go on the front of the jar.

DINNER IS SERVED

These are two menus for when you feel like giving your parents a day off. You can follow these instructions to produce an entire lunch or dinner on your own, emerging from the kitchen calm and in control knowing that a smashing meal is ready for eating.

MENU 1

DINNER FOR 4

Chicken with lemon and tarragon
Rice with toasted almonds
Mixed Green Salad
Chocolate Refrigerator Cake

Chicken with Lemon and Tarragon

EQUIPMENT

plate, frying pan, casserole dish with a lid, grater, lemon squeezer, scales, measuring jug

INGREDIENTS

4	chicken portions	4
50g	butter	2oz
50g	flour	2oz
1	lemon	1
2teasp	tarragon	2teasp
275ml	dry cider *or* chicken stock	½ pint
150ml	soured cream	¼ pint
	salt and pepper	

METHOD

1. Sprinkle the flour onto a plate and then season it with a pinch of salt and three good shakes of pepper.
2. Dip the four chicken pieces in the seasoned flour one by one so they are properly coated.
3. Melt the butter gently in a frying pan, then fry the chicken pieces on both sides till browned. Transfer them to a casserole dish.
4. Add the cider or stock, tarragon, the juice and finely grated rind of the lemon. Put the lid on the casserole.
5. Cook at Gas Mark 4 (350°F 180°C) till the chicken is tender — about an hour.
6. Take the casserole out of the oven and stir in the soured cream. Put back in the oven for 10 minutes to heat through just before serving, making sure you don't boil the sauce.

Rice with Toasted Almonds

EQUIPMENT

large saucepan, colander, clean tea towel, small frying pan, scales

INGREDIENTS

225g	long grain rice	8oz
50g	flaked almonds	2oz

METHOD

1. Bring a large pan of salted water to the boil and put in the rice.
2. Bring back to the boil, then turn down and simmer for 12 minutes. Take off the heat and drain through a colander. Put the rice back in the saucepan and tuck a clean tea towel over it to keep the steam in. Put back the lid. This finishes cooking the rice and gives you perfect separate grains.
3. Heat the sliced almonds carefully in a small heavy pan with no fat, shaking them about for a minute so they brown but don't burn. Scatter over the rice before serving.

Mixed Green Salad

Fresh and crisp

EQUIPMENT

kitchen paper, sharp knife, bowl, chopping board, tablespoon (tblsp)

INGREDIENTS

1 round lettuce
1 green pepper
½ cucumber
8 spring onions
4 tblsp vinaigrette (see p. 22)

METHOD

1. Remove the outer leaves of the lettuce, look carefully over the others and wash and dry them clean with kitchen paper. Place in a large salad bowl.
2. Cut the pepper in half lengthways and remove the stalk and seeds. Cut the flesh into strips. Add to the bowl.
3. Cut the cucumber into chunks leaving the skin on. Add to the bowl.
4. Trim the spring onions and cut off the roots. You can either leave the onions whole or cut into chunks. Add to the bowl.
5. Mix everything in the bowl together.
6. Add the dressing just before serving and toss the salad to make sure everything is coated with the dressing.

Chocolate Refrigerator Cake

You need to make this crunchy cake the day before so that it has 12 hours to chill in the fridge.

EQUIPMENT

small saucepan, small bowl, tablespoon, Loose bottomed 15cm (6 inch) cake tin, scales, serving plate

INGREDIENTS

150g	plain chocolate	6oz
125g	butter	5oz
1	egg	1
25g	caster sugar	1oz
150g	Digestive, Marie	6oz
	or	
	Butter Osborn biscuits	

METHOD

1. Very gently melt the butter and chocolate together in a saucepan over low heat.
2. Beat the egg and sugar together in a bowl till foamy, then gradually add the chocolate mixture.
3. Break the biscuits up into small pieces and stir in.
4. Grease a 15cm (6 inch) loose bottomed cake tin. Tip in the mixture and press it well down.
5. Chill in the fridge overnight.
6. Turn out on to a plate the next day.

MENU 2

SUNDAY LUNCH FOR 4

Roast Beef   Roast Potatoes   Gravy
Hannah's Yorkshire Pudding
Glazed Carrots
Apple Juice Jelly with fresh pears

COOKING TIME FOR BEEF

Roast Beef and Yorkshire Pudding are cooked at Gas Mark 6 (400°F 200°C). To work out the cooking time weigh the beef, then cook for 20 minutes per ½kg (1lb) plus an extra 20 minutes. A 1½kg (3lbs) roasting joint will take just under 1½ hours.

Roast Beef and Roast Potatoes

EQUIPMENT

2 roasting tins, tablespoon (tblsp), scales, sharp knife, chopping board, measuring jug, potato peeler, colander, patty tin or 20cm (8 inch) square tin, 2 bowls, wooden spoon, meat platter, vegetable dish, gravy boat or jug, cup

INGREDIENTS

1½kg	joint of roasting beef	3lbs
	pepper	
2tblsp	dripping	2tblsp
700g	potatoes	1½lbs
4tblsp	dripping	4tblsp

METHOD

1. Pre-heat the oven to Gas Mark 6 (400°F 200°C).
2. Weigh the joint and work out the cooking time if the piece of meat you have is more, or less than 1½kg (3lbs).
3. Wipe the meat with a clean damp cloth and sprinkle with pepper.
4. Melt the 2 tablespoons of dripping in a roasting tin, put in the meat, then baste with a little dripping. Cook as above.

ROAST POTATOES

1. Peel the potatoes and cook them in boiling salted water for 10 minutes. Take off the heat, and drain through a colander.
2. Melt the 4 tablespoons of dripping in a roasting tin.
3. When it is hot, remove the tin from the oven and put the potatoes in. Cook in the oven on the shelf below the meat. Baste occasionally.

Gravy

When the meat is cooked, transfer it to a serving dish and keep warm on top of the cooker while you make the gravy.

INGREDIENTS

1tblsp	flour	1tblsp
425ml	beef stock	¾ pint
	salt and pepper	
	fat from the roasting pan.	

METHOD

1. Pour off all but about 2 tablespoons of the fat in the meat roasting pan, leaving behind all the meat juices to give the gravy a delicious taste.
2. Stir in the flour, then put the pan over low heat on the top of the cooker.
3. Gradually add the stock (made from a cube) then the salt and pepper and, stirring all the time, bring the gravy to the boil. Continue cooking till slightly thickened. Pour into gravy boat or jug.

Hannah's Yorkshire Pudding

Put this into the oven 40 minutes before the end of the cooking time for the beef.

INGREDIENTS

100g	plain flour	4oz
	good pinch of salt	
2	eggs	2
275ml	milk	½ pint

METHOD

1. Sift the flour and salt into a bowl.
2. Break the eggs into a cup.
3. Make a well in the middle of the flour and add the eggs.
4. Gradually beat the flour into the eggs using a wooden spoon, adding half the milk as you go so the mixture won't be too thick to beat. Keep beating till you have a creamy batter. Stir in the rest of the milk.
5. In a pre-heated oven Gas Mark 6 (440°F 200°C, the oven will already be this hot if you're cooking the beef at the same time) first melt a little dripping in the holes of a patty tin for individual puddings, or in an 20cm (8 inch) square tin if you want a big billowing pud.
6. When the dripping begins to smoke, carefully lift the tin out of the oven, put it on a heatproof surface and pour in the batter. If you're using a patty tin, fill the holes 2/3 full.
7. Bake for 35 — 40 minutes on the shelf above the meat till the pudding is crisp, puffed up and golden brown.

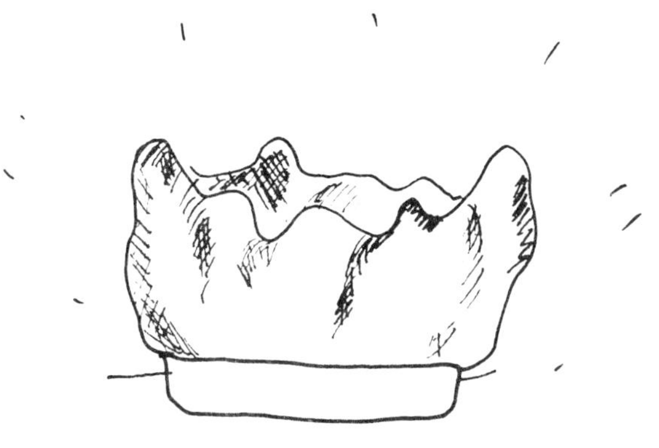

Glazed Carrots

EQUIPMENT

sharp knife, teaspoon (teasp), chopping board, scales, serving dish

INGREDIENTS

500g	carrots	1lb
	water	
½	chicken stock cube	½
1	walnut sized knob of butter	1
2teasp	sugar	2teasp

METHOD

1. Scrub the carrots and cut into sticks as thick as a pencil and as long as a thumb.
2. Put in a pan and just cover with water. Add the ½ stock cube, sugar and butter. Bring to the boil, then turn down to simmer till the liquid is absorbed and the carrots are shiny and tender.
3. Put in a serving dish.

Apple Jelly with Fresh Pears

make this in advance and put in the fridge

EQUIPMENT

small bowl, small saucepan, sharp knife, chopping board, jelly mould, plate, measuring jug, tablespoon

INGREDIENTS

400ml	apple juice	¾ pint
2	ripe fresh pears	2
	or	
	other fresh fruit in season (apples, bananas, melon, etc)	
1	sachet gelatine	1

METHOD

1. Melt the gelatine in 3 tablespoons of apple juice in a bowl over a saucepan of simmering water.
2. Stir in the rest of the apple juice and set aside to cool down.
3. Cut the pears into quarters and remove the cores. Slice the flesh thinly.
4. Stir into the jelly mixture, pour into a mould and leave in the fridge to set.
5. Turn out on a pretty plate.

INDEX